EVEN WITH CLIMATE CHANGE HAIKU

the days are still flush
with shivering spring again
the days go cooly

STUPID ME HAIKU

i stumble these days
wait stupidly to die here
happy i am now

UNLUCKY SPRING HAIKU

the days pass from dawn
till the music of nighttime
i hum poems waiting

THE MARROW BLEEDS TO SEED HAIKU

waking slowly now
a third time in the morning
over a cup of brew

SPRING LULLABY HAIKU

the days warn slowly
even now from chill to heat
the porch is stunning

MARCH 25TH HAIKU

the warm sunlight creeps
through morning portals it flows
to the forest floor

LOVE AND NATURE

these broken twigs show
the rustic signs of my heart
...my love is wooded

COUNTRY GIRL HAIKU

you are sweetest song
heart of the farm and forest
for you i live, die

SPRING SINGS SILLY HAIKU

hear the water lap
the shores of the melted lake
....with only kisses

BRSK LOGIC HAIKU

one step at a time
toward where the bottom leads to
at the end of it

BRISK NONSENSE HAIKU

walk rapidly nowhere
on nothingness crazy sore
with memories gone

SPRING SHIVERS HAIKU

early dawn we wake
the sunlight creeps upon us
outside the porch door

WINDMILLS HAIKU

windmills make movement
for power from the ocean
far out in the waves

THE PROBLEM HAIKU

i was born wrongly
some part of me was dumb then
...unable to speak

WHAT STRANGE THING HAIKU

what strange thing was it?
that caused my collapse these years
...strange thing forgotten

I AM HAPPY HAIKU

i am happy now
live well with my confusion
in this strange country

THE TRAGIC HEART LAUGHS HAIKU

here in old age laugh
like us god laughs just as well
all night by the fire

EACH BLADE OF GRASS HAIKU

life and death in each
in each stringy blade of grass
...stand up and laugh now

JOY HAIKU

music and nature
fill the world the trees, oceans
flood my heart with love

DESCENT HAIKU

down we went enjoined
to the basement of our love
to stare at ourselves

FRONTAL LABOTOMY HAIKU

as i age dull mind
i grow pacific inside
...waddle in the sun

WE SMILE ACHING HAIKU

laughter falls upon us
with our pain...is part of age
this way of our lives

PUSHING LIKE NAKED SPRING HAIKU

root to bud this time
innocent and stubbornly
i fallow downward

THE STUPID WAYS WE LOVE HAIKU

simple and singular
dully straight toward your heart
i give you my gift

STILL SHIVERIG HAIKU

winter keeps a cold
eye on the paths that i take
blows to let me know

SEEDS HAIKU

they are put away
in the soil and forgotten
until fall darkens

AFTERNOON HAIKU

the hot buttery
sunlight of a late mid-spring day
made me so sleepy

APRIL IS A CURSE HAIKU

april is a curse
made to crucify small gods
..weak, they drown always

NAKED REMNANTS HAIKU

not from the bath but
from winter's trees clawing out
the earth in springtime

STEWING HAIKU

only music calms
in this cycle of pure nerves
no cigarettes now

DAYS OF WONDERFUL NOTHIING HAIKU

nothing happens now
...this day yawns and streches out
like a fat balloon

EASING CLOUDY HAIKU

it looks to be rain
this pain of our struggling
underneath the sky

TEARS OF APRIL HAIKU

april rains in earnest
weeps like a mourning mother
all day long today

THE HARBOR OF MY HEART HAIKU

she who swells embracing
me and joking like smoke, fire,
...we laugh eternal

ANGELS RISE HAIKU

we see them streak up
like fire in the night they rise
while we watch sitting

SIGHS OF APRIL HAIKU

easter blesses us
the god who would return and
seek us in the flesh

HUMAN PIG HAIKU

the dire sense of night
...two a.m. and jam and toast
...the belly swells up

HUMAN PIG 2 HAIKU

wishing the fat would
melt away at two a.m.
...a sick way to die

HUMAN PIG 3 HAIKU

stareing at the black
pit of our dreams much like pork
roasting on a skewer

TREPIDATIONS HAIKU

Spring seems to be slow
the death of global warming
we   aimless wander

THE BEAUTY OF THE DEAD HAIKU

We are so human
tragiically woven the way
...there is no other

MY LOVER SHOULD LIVE HAPPY HAIKU

and her children also
she is more precious than these
useless tears we weep

HAPPY AND DEPRESSED HAIKU

we move slowly now
laughing moodily at dry
facts as they approach

THE HOURS ARE LONG AND SHORT HAIKU

long hours pass..we wait
for some sudden tradgedy
there are manny now

THE MIND KNOWS HOPE HAIKU

although. senselessly
we destroy our future, we
do not beilve it

REPUBLICANS HAIKU

fascists junk the earth
the planet is their garbage
nature dies...kills them

REPUBLICANS 2 HAIKU

the earth is a meal
made for the fat and greedy
they eat it and die

REPUBLICANS 3 HAIKU

bit coin rules the world
destroys it with methane too
we are rich with death

BREAKDOWN HAIKU

car trouble came on
a few days ago with us
cabin bound we are

BREAKDOWN 2 Haiku

my mnd is squeezed here
i pace the floors neurotic
...tense i pace the floors

BREAKDOWN 3 HAIKU

at night i am scarred
by the way the world goes on
sleep less...pace the floors

LONG PANTS IN SPRING HAIKU

morning is still cold
i shiver on the porch chair
stare off distantly

WORRYING TOO MUCH HAIKU

things are bad on earth
wars and climate change as well
...i crawl into shade

NERVOUS SLEEPNG HAIKU

i am barely awke
in the midst of dreaming on
nightmares...sick ending

NERVOUS SLEEPING 2 HAIKU

instead i am woke
but miserabley so this time
...opiim seems nice

NERVOUS SLEEPING 3 HAIKU

shallow sleep snoring
in the pit of my stomach
while i wish to drowse

END OF THE WORLD HAIKU

war, pestilence, plague
flood and drought as well begin
too fast...the ways down

END OF THE WORLD 2 HAIKU

but this has happened
before and too much again
nobody believes

STARE AT THE TV HAIKU

boring distractions
and the horror showas well
it could be blankness

HOWEVER LONG HAIKU

however long we
last, let us love forever
with our kiss and sigh

NATURE STIILL CALMS HAIKU

the waterfalls sound
...the wind touches us as well
.....things are brief, easy

BRIEF AND EASY HAIKU

I do weep for loss
but have little more to do

beside my vote now

GOOD FRIDAYING HAIKU

nails and shivering
terror matched by pain as well
and abandonment

GRAY GHOST OF SATURDAY HAIKU

the deep pit of sleep
surrounds of every intent
...piteous sleep too

THE EASTER OF EVERYTHING HAIKU

this is all of it
this is the tomb of jesus
our halelujahs

PORCUPINE HAIKU

hungry and numb here
...i swell in the belly's grip
inhaling food stuffs

PORCUPINE 2 HAIKU

my needles are sharo
but insciincually poised
to stupidly strike

PORCUPINE 3 HAIKU

i am used to it
indifferant now i munch
peaefully of food

THE END HAIKU

i try to eat less
drink and smoke nothing as well
nature is gorgeous

THE END 2 HAIKU

there may be war now
for all of us on the earth
at such a harsh time

THE END 3 HAIKU

we warm to a flood
we burn to a fire as well
in these fat days now

WHEN WE DIE HAIKU

when we pass does the
ghost of our ashes rise up
to god like a kiss

WHEN WE DIE 2 HAIKU

i hope my lover
will live forever she is
so good and sweet too

WHEN WE DIE 3 HAIKU

we are dust, trembling
in a bin and spill to mix
with the waters here

SPRING DAYS HAIKU

april has born light
on wooded acres in the day
and tvs at night

SPRING DAYS 2 HAIKU

trying to thin down
as the warm days come to us
sitting on a porch

SPRING DAYS 3 HAIKU

things are beautiful
as they disappear with heat
...coal and oil burning

RAPID FIRE HAIKU

machine guns rattle
nerves fly in the kitchen of
my hungry eating

RAPID FIRE 2 HAIKU

machine guns firing
bombs blasting orphans' mothers
the fascist onslaught

RAPID FIRE 3 HAIKU

stuccato bullets
in air void of life, and so
winning seems empty

www.ingramcontent.com/pod-product-compliance
Lightning Source LLC
Chambersburg PA
CBHW080731120726
48001CB00010B/3194